FINDING JOY ON THE BROKEN ROAD

A 31 DAY DEVOTIONAL

By Felicia J. Badger

Edited by Carol Medders

DEDICATION

This devotional is dedicated to Jesus. He alone has helped
me on my broken road. Whether through people, His Word,
or the Holy Spirit, He has always been present. His grace
has been sufficient in all situations, and He has provided
new mercies every day. May this devotional glorify Him
and help others find His joy on the broken road of life.

ACKNOWLEDGEMENT

This devotion was inspired by the Holy Spirit. I began writing in obedience, and when I put the 'pen to the paper,' the Holy Spirit would meet me. It was as if He was sharing with me the personal lives of His people and the healing He is bringing. He wants to restore your joy.

I want to thank my husband, for always being my encouragement and having faith that inspires. To my children and grandchildren, God has used you all to bring me comfort and joy in ways you will never know.

Thank you to my parents, who have stood by me on the road, even when I have broken it myself. God has shown me the depth of love through you all. Thank you to my little sister, who has been a joy for most of my life (LOL) and a champion for me!

Thank you to my best friend, Tiffany Blackshear. This road has had so much more joy and hope because of you being on it with me.

I want to acknowledge a few sisters in the Lord that God has used in remarkable ways to take my faith to new levels and inspire me for the 'more.' They unknowingly served as the catalyst for this Jesus project.

My "big sister" and mentor Cathy Gibson (Block). I love you and thank you for sowing joy in all my seasons. God has used you to grow my confidence in the woman He has called me to be, far greater than I could see in myself.

Susan Harkins, thank you for sharing a new level of faith with me and helping me realize that I am a 'facilitator' for Christ in more than one way.

I want to thank my sister and friend in Christ, Carol Medders. Your authenticity, kindness, and generosity have restored hope and sparked new faith in my soul. Even more, it was in the moment you offered to be my editor, that I realized God had a bigger plan for this book.

INTRODUCTION

No matter how long you have been a Christian, you will have to navigate various trials (Ps 34:19.) The purpose of this devotional is to acknowledge the road we walk on is broken, but joy is ours to have if we choose. Finding joy comes from intentionality and a purposeful change in perspective.

Join the Holy Spirit on this 31 day journey. Each day in this devotional is designed to shift your perspective by providing foundational scriptures and a relatable story to connect with. Additionally, there is a section called "Faith by Works" (James 2:18) which gives a practical way to understand and apply the wisdom. Every entry concludes with a declaration for you to speak out loud...because there is power in proclaiming the Word of God over your life (Is 55:11, Heb 4:12, Pro 18:21.)

OVERCOMING FEAR

Isaiah 41:10 – Fear not, for I am with you...

2 Timothy 1:7 – For God has not given us a spirit of fear, but of power, love and a sound mind.

Janet was scheduled for a major surgery. Every night she was taunted with fear filled thoughts, keeping her awake. One night she realized in all her fearful nights she never prayed. As soon as Janet prayed she felt an inexplicable peace wash over her. On the day of surgery, the nurse took Janet by the hand and prayed with her. Janet was filled with joy and peace as she felt God's presence around her.

FAITH BY WORKS

What fears have been taunting you? Taunting and fear are weapons the enemy uses to isolate, distract, and rob us of God's peace and joy. Remember to pray and release your fears to God. His perfect love casts out fear and His Spirit brings peace beyond understanding.

DECLARATION

I break off every agreement I made with fear and declare that God has given me a spirit of power, love, and a sound mind in Jesus' Name.

ENDURING THROUGH CHRONIC ILLNESS

2 Corinthians 12:9 – My grace is sufficient for you, for My strength is made perfect in weakness.

Psalm 73:26 – My flesh and my heart may fail, but God is the strength of my heart...

Jeremy struggles daily with chronic pain. One day, he decided to volunteer at a local shelter despite his own limitations. In this small act of service, he began to feel purpose and joy beyond his pain. By stepping out and serving others, God shifted Jeremy's focus from suffering to purpose.

FAITH BY WORKS

Even in our weakness and suffering, God's strength and purpose can shine through us. Ask God how you can serve, where you can serve, and who you serve. Even in your suffering, you possess the ability to give hope to others, you have purpose. Our lives are made of many seasons. When your season changes in life, it's a good time to seek God about His purpose for you to ensure you are on the same page! God uses our weakness to reveal His greatest strength.

DECLARATION

Thank you that your grace is sufficient. God use my suffering and weakness for Your purpose and glory in Jesus' Name.

OVERCOMING REJECTION

Psalm 27:10 – When my father and my mother forsake me, then the Lord will take care of me.

Romans 8:38-39 – For I am persuaded that neither death nor life...shall be able to separate us from the love of God which is in Christ Jesus our Lord.

When I was going through my divorce, I remember feeling so rejected and abandoned by those I called friends in ministry. One day during a walk, I began to cry out to God about how I felt, devastated and hurt by these people and "after all I'd done for them." At that moment I heard the Lord say, "How do you think I felt on the cross?" The Lord reminded me that I was not alone and that He truly understood how I felt. I was instantly filled with peace. God used that moment to help me forgive them and not allow roots of bitterness to take hold.

FAITH BY WORKS

God also faced rejection by those close to Him. Ask God to uproot any seeds of bitterness and to show you who you need to forgive. Rejection from others does not diminish your value in God's eyes. Remember He will never abandon you.

DECLARATION

I forgive all those that have rejected, betrayed, and abandoned me and declare I am healed and perfect in my father's eyes.

FINDING JOY IN GRIEF

Psalm 34:18 – The Lord is near to those who have a broken heart...

Matthew 5:4 – Blessed are those who mourn, for they shall be comforted.

After losing her spouse, Bailey struggled to find meaning in her daily life. One heavy day, she noticed a flower blooming outside her window—a small, beautiful reminder of life. In that moment, she realized that even in her deepest pain, God was with her, comforting her and guiding her to find moments of joy.

FAITH BY WORKS

Grieving loss is natural. Sometimes the only constant is the unpredictability of your emotions. Navigating a new routine is challenging and can lead us down many dark paths. God can bring comfort through small reminders that He hasn't left us alone in our sorrow. Be intentional about looking at your surroundings. Nature or even those around you can provide a glimpse of light and beauty. If we don't take moments to be intentional, we can easily get stuck in the dark.

DECLARATION

God, thank you for being here in my deepest sorrows and helping me still find joy. You comfort me in my brokenness, and I find light in moments of darkness.

HOPE FOR THE HOPELESS

Lamentations 3:22-23 – Through the Lord's mercies we are not consumed, because His compassions fail not. They are new every morning.

Isaiah 40:31 – But those who wait on the Lord shall renew their strength...

Grant has been struggling to find a job for months after being laid off. Just when he's about to lose hope, a neighbor drops off a meal for his family, reminding him that God shows His presence in small acts of kindness. Grant's hope is restored through this divine intervention. Even in times of despair, God is working for you, and can work unexpectedly through others.

FAITH BY WORKS

If your hope is fading, take the time today to look at how God's hand has previously moved for you. Encourage your soul that He is the same God today. If you are feeling full of hope today, do a small act of kindness to stir up the hope again in a friend. Hope appears through the smallest of gestures by showing God's love.

DECLARATION

God, you are faithful! I break off a spirit of hope deferred and declare the God of hope is filling me with joy and peace in Jesus' Name.

FINDING JOY THROUGH FORGIVENESS

Colossians 3:13 – Bear with each other and forgive one another... Forgive as the Lord forgave you.

Matthew 6:14 – For if you forgive others their trespasses, your heavenly Father will also forgive you.

Renee has been holding onto anger toward a friend for months. The enemy has convinced her that she is entitled to be angry toward her friend. Every time something reminds her of the friend, those feelings of anger arise, provoking her all over again. One day, as she is reading in her Bible, the Lord brings her to a passage about forgiveness. As she reads over it, she receives revelation and conviction in her spirit. Unforgiveness was disguised as 'righteous anger.' How could she expect God to forgive her for everything when she doesn't deserve it, but she was not willing to forgive her friend? She immediately forgave her friend in her heart and asked God to forgive her. Even if they never reconcile, Renee has chosen to forgive. She feels the weight lift off her and experiences fresh joy.   11

FAITH BY WORKS

Emotions are just the flags for a rooted issue. Renee was walking in a lie of "righteous anger," when in reality she was rooted in unforgiveness. God speaks to us through His Word. Forgiveness is always a choice and it is an intentional choice that affects our walk with God more than it affects the other person. There is freedom and joy that come when you make a conscious decision to forgive someone, even if they don't deserve it. Afterall, we don't deserve all that Jesus did for us. Additionally, God has given us the commandment to "forgive one another." Ask God to search your heart for hidden unforgiveness and to show you hidden roots. If you are struggling to forgive someone, ask God, "Give me the desire to forgive ____, for I know that is your will."

DECLARATION

I forgive others, as Christ has forgiven me. God gives me revelation when I read His Word. I declare all roots of unforgiveness are uprooted right now and replaced with fresh joy in Jesus' Name!

TRUSTING GOD IN THE UNKNOWN

Psalms 37:5 – Commit your way to the Lord, trust also in Him, and He shall bring it to pass.

Hebrews 11:1 – Now faith is the substance of things hoped for, the evidence of things not seen.

Jane finally received the opportunity she had been waiting for and accepted a new job in a new city. While preparing to move she was filled with anxiety about the change and leaving her support network. As these fleeting thoughts came, she prayed asking God to guide her steps and thanked Him for leading her through this new opportunity. As Jane followed her path, God was faithful to connect her to a new church, friendly neighbors, and some encouraging coworkers.

FAITH BY WORKS

God's plan often involves steps of faith, and sometimes that means walking forward without having all the answers. Trust God's guiding hand as you walk down new paths.

DECLARATION

I declare I trust God leading my steps. I walk by faith and not by sight in Jesus' Name.

WATCHING LOVED ONES SUFFER

2 Corinthians 1:3-4 – ...the Father of mercies and God of all comfort, who comforts us in all our tribulation...

Romans 8:18 – For I consider that the sufferings of this present time are not worthy to be compared with the glory which shall be revealed...

Pam had felt so helpless as she watched her best friend battle cancer. Her prayers had been focused solely on healing until the Holy Spirit nudged her to pray for peace and joy on the journey as well. Pam was surprised by how quickly the atmosphere changed and more moments of laughter were shared. These moments reminded her that God brings joy and connection, even in dark times, strengthening her friendship in ways she never expected.

FAITH BY WORKS

God is the Great Comforter. Ask God what He wants you to pray for your loved ones. His perspective and understanding are far greater than ours. Even when you can't change a loved one's situation, your support and prayers can bring peace and a gentle joy that reflects God's love.

DECLARATION

God, you are the Great Comforter, my comforter. The atmosphere changes when I speak and my prayers bring peace and joy!

FINDING JOY IN SMALL BLESSINGS

Philippians 4:4 – Rejoice in the Lord always. Again I will say, rejoice!

James 1:17 – Every good gift and every perfect gift is from above, and comes down from the Father of lights...

In the midst of a busy day caring for her children, cleaning up spills, changing diapers, and tripping on a toy, Rochelle stumbles upon a moment of peace when her toddler suddenly hugs her leg tightly. This simple moment brings her joy and reminds her of the countless blessings God weaves into her busiest days.

FAITH BY WORKS

It can be very easy on our busiest days to notice the small blessings God has placed. In fact, sometimes we can even mistake them as an inconvenience. Be even more purposeful in the rush to acknowledge small blessings. It could be a smile, it may be the presence or absence of someone, or just the right timing. Everyday God has blessings for you and with you in mind.

DECLARATION

God gives me good and perfect gifts. I rejoice in the Lord always. I recognize the blessings of God in my life in Jesus' Name.

TRUSTING GOD TO HEAL WHAT'S BROKEN

Psalm 147:3 – He heals the brokenhearted and binds up their wounds.

Romans 12:18 – If it is possible, as much as depends on you, live peaceably with all men.

Mandy has been devastated after having to end her friendship with a close friend. Brokenhearted, she begins to experience the emotions of grief. She wrestles with feelings of anger and loss. As she begins to get worked back up again, she prays. By acknowledging God during her brokenness, she feels God inviting her to release her pain to Him. Not knowing exactly how to do that, she mutters out, "God take this pain from me." Slowly, she begins to feel His peace fill her heart. While the friendship may never be the same, Mandy feels comforted knowing that God is close. This brings her hope and restores joy in her heart.

FAITH BY WORKS

Even in our brokenness, God can restore joy to us, piece by piece. Today, bring your pain, grief, and brokenness caused by people and relationships to God. Ask Him to, "Take this pain away from me." Pause to feel God's presence and heart around you, as you surrender the pain of loss for the healing that God's presence brings. He will bring restoration to your soul in ways you have never imagined.

DECLARATION

God has healed my broken heart. I release all pain, anger, and bitterness to you Lord. I declare that I have perfect peace and my joy has been restored in Jesus' Name!

THE UNEXPECTED GIFT OF PATIENCE

Proverbs 16:32 – Better to be patient than powerful; better to have self-control than to conquer a city.

Galatians 5:22 – But the fruit of the Spirit is love, joy, peace, patience...

Sarah was waiting in the carpool line while her toddler was screaming in the backseat, bored out of his mind. She reached for her phone to distract him, but it was dead. Instead of yelling back, she started making silly faces and voices. Before she knew it, they were both cracking up. In that moment, she realized that patience (and a good sense of humor) can turn even carpool chaos into unexpected joy.

FAITH BY WORKS

Life gives us plenty of opportunities to practice patience. We have the choice in any situation on how to respond, choosing to be patient or impatient. When you have to make the choice today, choose patience and experience joy in the waiting, instead of chaos. Your 'level' of patience is a gauge for your level of submission to God's timing. If you lose your patience today, be humble enough to apologize and be ready to succeed the next time.

DECLARATION

I have patience because it is a fruit of the spirit. I am patient with others and make joyful moments in the waiting.

DAY 12

JOY IN THE MESS

Ecclesiastes 3:12-13 – I know that there is nothing better for people than to be happy and to do good while they live.

Psalm 118:24 – This is the day the Lord has made; we will rejoice and be glad in it.

Tanisha is frantically cleaning up her house for guests when her toddler decides to "help" by dumping a bag of flour on the floor. She's about to lose it when her son grabs a handful of flour, throws it in the air, and says, "Snow mommy!" In that moment, she can't help but laugh, realizing life's messes sometimes bring the most memorable joy.

FAITH BY WORKS

Find the joy in life's unexpected messes. God sometimes uses the things that interrupt our plans to sprinkle joy and remind us of life's playful side.

DECLARATION

I break off a spirit of heaviness and replace it with a garment of praise in Jesus' Name!

THE BEAUTY OF AN AFTERNOON NAP

Matthew 11:28 – Come to Me, all you who labor and are heavy laden, and I will give you rest.

Psalm 4:8 – I will both lie down in peace, and sleep; for You alone, O Lord, make me dwell in safety.

Grandad Dan was known for his daily "power nap." The whole family laughed at his dedication to these naps, as he never missed one. One day, his granddaughter joined him on the couch and fell asleep beside him. When she woke up, she realized napping is a form of rest. Slowing down to enjoy God's ordained rest can bring a quick restoration to a busy soul.

FAITH BY WORKS

Rest is a gift from God and also a commandment. God himself rested on the seventh day and we see Jesus rested in the Bible as well. It is difficult to experience joy when you are exhausted. While everyone can't take a nap today, you can take a few minutes in the middle of your day and pause. Close your eyes, take a few deep breaths in and allow the Holy Spirit to breathe on you and refresh your joy.

DECLARATION

I declare that God is my resting place and I make time to rest in Him.

DANCING LIKE NO ONE'S WATCHING

Psalm 30:11 – You have turned for me my mourning into dancing...

Zephaniah 3:17 – The Lord your God in your midst... will rejoice over you with gladness...

Hailey is in the grocery store, earbuds in, when her favorite song comes on. Not realizing the cashier is watching, she begins to dance to the rhythm, until she notices he is smiling at her. Embarrassed, she laughs, but then the cashier begins to dance. They both enjoy a lighthearted moment, and she realizes that God's joy can reach us anywhere—even the grocery store.

FAITH BY WORKS

Find God's joy in everyday places today and embrace spontaneous moments of happiness without worrying who's watching. Life is full of small reasons to dance, even in a grocery store!

DECLARATION

I declare you have turned my mourning to dancing and you rejoice over me with gladness in Jesus' Name

FROM FRUSTRATION TO GRATITUDE

1 Thessalonians 5:18 – In everything give thanks; for this is the will of God in Christ Jesus for you.

Colossians 3:17 – And whatever you do, in word or deed, do all in the name of the Lord Jesus, giving thanks to God...

After his sixth 12 hour shift, Bryan is grumbling about having to fix the leaky faucet on his day off, frustrated by yet another chore. As he kneels down under the sink to tighten the pipes, the Lord brings back the memory of when his father taught him these skills. Recalling this changes a frustrating chore into a moment of gratitude. Bryan begins to thank God for his father, the house, the faucet, and skills he has to fix it himself.

FAITH BY WORKS

As you see inconveniences in your situation today, shift your focus to the hidden blessing. What can you thank God for? God is always speaking to us and will use moments to open our eyes to the many gifts we sometimes overlook.

DECLARATION

I give thanks to God for every day and every situation. All that I do, I do in the name of Jesus, giving thanks to God who is the author and finisher of my faith.

SEEING THE BLESSING IN INTERRUPTIONS

Proverbs 16:9 – A man's heart plans his way, but the Lord directs his steps.

Romans 8:28 – And we know that all things work together for good to those who love God...

Huong was stressed because she was running late to work and it seemed everything that could go wrong, went wrong. In her hustle to the door, a man stopped her and asked for help after dropping his bag. Though she was annoyed, she stopped to assist him. While thanking her, he shared he was on the way to visit his wife in the hospital. At that moment, she realized her day's "delay" was nothing compared to being in the hospital. God was giving her an opportunity to be a blessing to someone in greater need.

FAITH BY WORKS

A pastor of mine would say, "Blessed are the flexible, for they won't be bent out of shape!" Often we are so focused on the inconvenience that interrupted our plans, we overlook that God is working through them. The next time your plan is interrupted, ask God, "Is there something I need to do here? What do you want me to see?" Trust that God has a purpose for all things and is directing your path.

DECLARATION

I decree that my path, my time, and my steps are directed by you. I submit to your perfect will and declare that everything is working out for my good because I love you and am called according to your purpose in Jesus' Name.

CONTENTMENT IN THE MUNDANE

Philippians 4:11 – ...for I have learned in whatever state I am, to be content.

1 Timothy 6:6 – Now godliness with contentment is great gain.

Miguel didn't mind sharing house chores, however, he dreaded doing laundry, "the ultimate 'boring' chore." Today while folding, he saw past the task and saw the blessing, as he was flooded with memories from each piece. He began to think about the shirt he wore to the family barbecue, the socks from hiking with friends, and towels from cooking with his daughter. He was filled with joy as he exchanged a household chore for gratitude.

FAITH BY WORKS

It is so easy to get caught up in everyday tasks that we lose the value in them. I remember when the loads were small and frequent because we didn't have enough clothes for each day of the week to now complaining about how much there is to fold! We must ask God to help us appreciate simple things and remind us that some of the things we are complaining about are the same things we once prayed to have. Shift your perspective to see the mundane tasks as a blessing rather than a burden and you will experience more joy in your life.

DECLARATION

I declare that I am content in all situations. The joy of the Lord is my strength and I count blessings rather than burdens in Jesus' Name.

EMBRACING THE PRESENT MOMENT

Matthew 6:34 – Therefore do not worry about tomorrow, for tomorrow will worry about its own things...

Psalm 16:11 – You will show me the path of life; in Your presence is fullness of joy...

Neidra was very focused on planning for the future, often causing stress. One evening, while watching a sunset with friends, a friend asked her what color in the sky she liked most. Neidra didn't even notice the different colors because her mind was thinking about everything she needed to do the next day. She realized she was missing the beauty of now. Neidra decided it was time to slow down and allow herself to be present in the present to enjoy each moment. This shift brought a sense of peace and contentment she hadn't felt in a long time.

FAITH BY WORKS

Today be intentional about slowing down to savor the present. God is in every moment, and we can find true joy by shifting our focus from what's ahead to what He's offering us right now. Despite planning ahead, what you sow now, you will reap later. If we neglect sowing into relationships now because we are busy planning the future, we will reap a future with poor relationships.

DECLARATION

I will not worry about tomorrow and will have fullness of joy in Your presence. I am sowing good seeds now that I will reap later.

SEEKING GOD IN HIS WORD

Psalm 119:105 – Your word is a lamp to my feet and a light to my path.

Joshua 1:8 – This Book of the Law shall not depart from your mouth, but you shall meditate in it day and night...

Robert feels lost and uncertain about his next steps in life. Even though he doesn't know exactly where to start, he turns to his bible and begins to spend a few minutes each morning reading God's Word. As he reads, passages begin speaking directly to his situation, providing clarity and comfort. He begins to realize that God's guidance is always there, waiting for him in His Word.

FAITH BY WORKS

Today, pray and ask God for some direction regarding what is on your heart. Then spend time reading God's word to watch Him speak directly to you. Even if you don't know where to begin, pray and then open your bible. Believe that you will start exactly where He wants you to. Have confidence that God speaks to us through His Word, offering guidance, comfort, and wisdom for each step.

DECLARATION

I will meditate on your word day and night for it is a lamp to my feet and light to my path! God's Word speaks to me!

FINDING FAMILY IN CHRIST'S LOVE

John 13:34-35 – A new commandment I give to you, that you love one another...

Psalm 68:6 – God sets the solitary in families...

Due to his faith walk, Javier feels disconnected from his family and decides to join a small group through his church. Although he is naturally an introvert, he finds others who can relate to him and encourage him in his faith. He connects with people who care for him and these new friends give him a sense of belonging. Although his family situation hasn't changed, having a family of believers has filled that void and allowed him to experience the love of Christ through the people around him.

FAITH BY WORKS

When you become a citizen of heaven, you can feel disconnected from others who are not on the same faith walk, or on the same level. God provides us community and family through the body of Christ. The bible also tells us to not forsake the assembling of ourselves together (Heb 10:25). If you haven't been in a church building in a while, it is time to get connected to the "family." All of us need to get connected with a small group that can help support us, help grow us and allow us to support others as the family of Christ.

DECLARATION

God has given me a family and I belong in the body of Christ. I love others and am loved. I create community and family wherever I go.

THE POWER OF PRAYER

Philippians 4:6-7 – Be anxious for nothing, but in everything by prayer and supplication, with thanksgiving, let your requests be made known to God...

James 5:16 – ...The effective, fervent prayer of a righteous man avails much.

After trying several different suggestions, Rachel continues struggling with anxiety and decides to start praying daily. Initially, it feels awkward and she's unsure if she's "doing it right." As she continues each day, she notices her worries slowly diminishing. Through prayer, she begins to feel God's peace in a new way. She's no longer carrying her burdens alone —she's placed them in God's hands and He is carrying the load.

FAITH BY WORKS

Prayer doesn't have to be perfect; it just needs to be sincere. Through prayer, we connect our hearts with God's and find a peace that only He can provide. Praying to God daily positions and prepares you for unplanned attacks from the enemy, it also allows God to put more of Him in you. Pray sincerely from your heart today and commit to daily prayer, even if it is 30 seconds!

DECLARATION

I bind up the spirit of anxiety and fear and break off every agreement in Jesus' Name. I declare that I have a peace that surpasses all understanding and my mind is in perfect peace because it is stayed upon Jesus.

BUILDING A RELATIONSHIP THROUGH REFLECTION

Psalm 1:2 – But his delight is in the law of the Lord, and in His law he meditates day and night.

Matthew 11:28 – Come to Me, all you who labor and are heavy laden, and I will give you rest.

Francis, a busy single mom, decides she wants to grow closer to God. Not having much time, she dedicates 5 minutes every night to reflecting on one Bible verse. By the end of the week, she can already sense her relationship with Jesus has grown closer and deeper. As she continues to record her reflections each night, she realizes that her ability to hear God's voice more clearly has improved and she looks forward to this daily encounter. Striving for more, she begins to carry the daily verse with her, allowing God to mold her perspective throughout the day.

FAITH BY WORKS

Today, make the decision to give God time daily. Maybe you have 5 minutes, maybe you only have 2, or maybe you are in a season to do more. It is not about the amount of time, it is about being purposeful in meeting with Jesus. None of us can grow in a relationship without putting in some time. To hear God's voice, we have to know his Word. During your time, pick one verse to reflect on.

DECLARATION

I draw near to God and He draws near to me. I meditate on your Word day and night and have hidden it in my heart that I might not sin against you.

THE JOY OF HEARING GOD'S VOICE

John 10:27 – My sheep hear My voice, and I know them, and they follow Me.

Jeremiah 33:3 – Call to Me, and I will answer you, and show you great and mighty things, which you do not know.

Javon spends time in prayer, asking God for direction but feeling unsure if he's "hearing" anything. One day after praying, he sits in quietness, waiting to hear God. A clear idea "just drops" into his mind. He knows immediately God is speaking to him. By recognizing and acknowledging this, Javon becomes confident that God does hear him and is guiding him along the path of life.

FAITH BY WORKS

God speaks to us in various ways, often through His Word and prayer. What have you been seeking God for? Today, find some time with no distractions to sit quietly at the feet of Jesus. Don't write off thoughts that just "drop" in, or a quiet voice that sounds like you. We are spiritual beings and God often speaks to us in the spirit, not an audible voice. Despite how you may feel, God desires to speak to you. You are His sheep, therefore it is a promise that you hear His voice.

DECLARATION

I am your sheep and I hear Your voice. I seek You and find You because I seek You with all my heart. You show me great and mighty things.

FINDING JOY IN GOD'S LOVE WHEN OTHERS LEAVE

Isaiah 41:10 – Fear not, for I am with you; be not dismayed, for I am your God.

John 14:18 I will not leave you orphans; I will come to you.

Michael has had a strained relationship with his family for years, but now they have cut off all contact with him. While his pride tells him, "you don't need them," in his heart he feels abandoned and betrayed. It hurts deeply, and he wonders if he'll ever find peace. For months he has masked and coped with his sorrow, but the bitterness and the restlessness has increased. Realizing he can't fix this feeling on his own, he turns to God in prayer. Confessing his feelings of bitterness, unforgiveness, and feeling abandoned, he begins to feel the Holy Spirit assuring him that he is not abandoned and God is with him. He realizes that God's love is steadfast. In reaching out to God, the feelings of bitterness and unforgiveness are uprooted and a peace that surpasses all understanding comes upon him. This brings him unexpected comfort and joy.

FAITH BY WORKS

Even when human relationships fail, God's love is constant and our relationship with Him will never fail. God promises that we will not be an orphan. We can only achieve true peace and joy when we trust God and invite Him to assist us. Today, reflect on your relationships with others. Confess how you truly feel to God, then invite God to intervene—not how you think it should be done, but truly saying, "Not my will, but Your will be done"

DECLARATION

I am not an orphan. God is always with me. I break off agreement with the strongholds of abandonment and bitterness. I forgive those that have hurt me as God has forgiven me.

BEAUTY FROM ASHES

Revelation 21:4 And God will wipe away every tear from their eyes; there shall be no more death, nor sorrow, nor crying...

Isaiah 61:3 To console those who mourn in Zion, to give them beauty for ashes, the oil of joy for mourning, the garment of praise for the spirit of heaviness; that they may be called trees of righteousness, the planting of the Lord, that He may be glorified.

Gabriella and her husband were overjoyed when they learned they were pregnant for the first time. Six weeks later, their joy was turned into sorrow when she had a miscarriage. Devastated, she struggles to understand why God would allow this to happen. She begins to meditate on God's word, focusing on Psalm 34:17-18.

In time she begins to find comfort in writing letters to her unborn child. As the letters build up, she decides to share them with other grieving mothers, to bring hope and encouragement. These letters eventually become a devotional book for other grieving mothers, showing them how God can bring beauty even from the ashes of loss.

FAITH BY WORKS

God will take our ashes (the loss, our brokenness) and turn them into beauty by redeeming those moments in a way that brings Him glory. If we place our sorrow, grief, pain, and brokenness in His hands, we will have a new hope and healing. Look at the ashes you have in life, reflect on how God has turned that for His glory. If God hasn't exchanged your ashes for beauty yet, ask Him.

DECLARATION

God has turned my mourning into dancing. He is near me. He has taken my ashes and turned them into beauty. I wear a garment of praise.

HOPE FOR RECONCILIATION

Matthew 5:9 – Blessed are the peacemakers, for they shall be called sons of God.

Colossians 3:13 – Bear with each other and forgive one another... as the Lord has forgiven you, so you also must forgive.

After a big fallout with her mother, Taylor hasn't spoken to her for years. She still loves her mom and misses her but doesn't know how their relationship can be repaired. Instead of allowing this pain to bring her down, she prays daily for her mother, asking God to soften both their hearts. One day, her mother reaches out, and together they begin a healing journey with God. She learns that with God, all things are possible. Even the most broken relationships can be restored.

FAITH BY WORKS

In the midst of brokenness, we are faced with making decisions. Do you believe that God is for you? Do you believe that all things are possible with God? The Bible is clear that our time and God's time are not the same. If you haven't sought God for the impossible, today is the day! Ask God to help soften both your hearts and to help you forgive. If you have been seeking reconciliation for a while now, do not lose heart! God is able and His timing is best. He is the Prince of Peace and through Him, relationships can be restored.

DECLARATION

I declare that God is for me and all things are possible with Him. He has healed my heart and I have joy and peace. My relationship with _____ is restored!

STRENGTH IN THE STRUGGLE

2 Corinthians 12:9 -And He said to me, 'My grace is sufficient for you, for My strength is made perfect in weakness.

Proverbs 3:5 Trust in the Lord with all your heart and lean not on your own understanding.

Ashley has lived with chronic back pain ever since her car accident. She has used therapy, medications, and other holistic efforts, but continues to battle pain daily. One day during her prayer time, she hears a still soft voice say, "My grace is sufficient for you." Ashley begins to understand, like Paul, that God is using her pain for His glory. She decides to partner with God and use her pain to encourage others. Ashley puts together a small support group for others that suffer with chronic pain. Through this group she brings hope and healing to others on the road.

FAITH BY WORKS

Most people do not choose the fruit of "long suffering," yet it is one of the fruits of the Spirit. Proverbs tells us to "Trust in the Lord with all our heart." It can be easy in the struggles of life, especially long term battles, to lose sight of God's grace and trust in His better plans. Yet, Jesus understands that and whispers to us, "My grace is sufficient." We too have the opportunity to take pain and suffering and turn it into purpose for God's glory. Think about how you can use your current pain or previous pain to encourage others.

DECLARATION

Lord, I trust you with all my heart. Your grace is sufficient. My life is a living testimony. Use me for your glory!

TURNING FRUSTRATION INTO PRAYER

Proverbs 14:29 – He who is slow to wrath has great understanding, but he who is impulsive exalts folly.

James 1:19-20 – So then, my beloved brethren, let every man be swift to hear, slow to speak, slow to wrath...

James is frustrated with his teenagers, and the tension is wearing him down. It takes everything in him this evening not to lash out. Beyond words, he goes and sits in his truck just to get away. As he reviews the situation, he decides to turn his frustration into prayer and shares his anger with God. At first he is talking, then ranting, then yelling to God. Like a flood, the calming presence of God falls on him unexpectedly. He begins to weep tears of joy and peace as he is comforted by the Spirit, knowing God hears and sees him.

FAITH BY WORKS

God is big enough for your anger! Just like we can bring our brokenness to God, we can bring our anger and frustration to God. In fact, He wants us to bring it to Him. If you will bring your moment of anger into a moment with God, you will be able to experience transformation from anger to peace and joy. That's right, even joy! Our Bible shows us that Jesus experienced anger and frustration (Matt 21:12-13). God understands us, He knows us, and as a father, He knows how to help us. There is great joy that comes from knowing that we can come as we are to a Father who will listen, love, and direct our paths.

DECLARATION

I am swift to hear, slow to speak and slow to wrath. I pray about all things and God hears and answers all my requests.

CHOOSING JOY OVER JUSTICE

Romans 12:19 – Beloved, do not avenge yourselves, but rather give no place to wrath; for it is written, "Vengeance is Mine, I will repay," says the Lord.

Proverbs 21:15 – It is a joy for the just to do justice, But destruction will come to the workers of iniquity.

Juan is angry after learning about a coworker unfairly taking credit for his work. He plans to confront his coworker. While preparing his attack, he decides to pray for wisdom regarding this injustice. As he prays, the Holy Spirit reminds him that God sees all injustices and that "Vengeance is Mine." In response, Juan asks God to help him trust in His plan and timing and releases his desire for "payback." Trusting God to balance the scale of justice, provides a freedom and joy that Juan did not anticipate.

FAITH BY WORKS

God is so amazing when we seek Him in prayer, He loves us enough to direct us to a greater wisdom and perspective. We all face situations of injustice and are tempted to "take care of it ourselves," but God's ways are not our ways (Is 55:8). Today is a day to choose joy instead of anger and release your need for justice to God. Trust that He is in control and has your best interest in mind. He is the God of justice and will balance the scale.

DECLARATION

You are the God of justice, and I trust You. I declare that You have balanced the scale of justice, and I have exchanged anger for joy in Jesus' Name!

THE JOY OF GOD'S UNFAILING LOVE

1 John 3:1 – Behold what manner of love the Father has bestowed on us, that we should be called children of God!

Psalm 103:13 – As a father has compassion on his children, so the Lord has compassion on those who fear him.

Shontell is struggling to find her identity. She feels lost and insecure. One evening, while reading her Bible, she begins to understand that identity has more to do with who we are, than what we do. She is God's beloved daughter and He loves her just for being His. The feelings of being insecure and lost fade. They are replaced with joy. She knows that no matter what she does or where she goes, His love for her is unwavering. Shontell realizes being a daughter of the King is her identity!

FAITH BY WORKS

God loves us so much that He died for us. There are not too many people that have proven their love for you to this level, especially death on the cross. Ask God to show you how He sees you. Ask Him to reveal His love for you in a new way. As you think about being His child, think about your identity and responsibility as a child of the King.

DECLARATION

I am a child of God. The Lord loves me and has compassion for me. I have a purpose. God will prosper me and not harm me, He gives me hope and a future.

GUIDED BY A FAITHFUL FATHER

Psalm 32:8 - I will instruct you and teach you in the way you should go; I will guide you with My eye.

Matthew 6:26 - Look at the birds of the air... Are you not of more value than they?

Cedric is overwhelmed by life's demands as a provider, father, and husband. He questions what his future looks like and is uncertain of the direction he needs to take. It has been a while, but he decides it is time to get alone with God. During his quiet moment, God reminds him that He orders Cedric's steps (Psalms 37:23) and directs his path (Proverbs 16:9). This assurance produces a peace and joy in him because he is not alone and the current demands are part of the path, not the final plan.

FAITH BY WORKS

Day to Day routine and demands can easily cause us to lose sight of the big picture. We change our focus from "this is the path He put me on," to the daily tasks at hand. We can forget altogether that God is still ordering our steps. Find joy in knowing that where we currently are is not our final destination. Take some quiet time with God, share your burdens and desire for guidance. Ask him to show you the bigger picture.

DECLARATION

God orders my steps and is directing my path! I have joy and peace resting in God's plan for me. He instructs me and teaches me the way to go.